Bitcoin Guide for Beginners

I0481608

How to Invest in Bitcoins to earn a profit in 1 hour

Table of Contents

Introduction

Thank you and congratulations for buying this book.

Bitcoins are rapidly becoming one of the most talked about topics of this year. Everywhere you go, people are either talking about buying Bitcoins, investing in them or selling them. However, this excessive coverage has also led to the spreading of various myths and legends about Bitcoins that are tarnishing the image of this highly secure and transparent currency. This book will try to do away with all such myths and will teach you how to invest in Bitcoins to earn a profit.

This book will serve as a guidebook for everyone who is interested in Bitcoins but does not know where to begin. In this book, you will learn the basics of cryptocurrencies and how they are better than fiat or normal currencies. You will also learn about the origin and history of Bitcoins and how they came into existence to change the history of the world.

In the 'how to' section of the book, you will learn about investing and buying Bitcoins and the different types of wallets that can be used to store them. You will also learn the basics of Bitcoin mining.

Lastly, this book will also deal with the advantages as well disadvantages of Bitcoins, which will allow you to invest in them safely.

Once again thank you for buying this book and now let us begin!

Chapter One: What is Cryptocurrency?

Before beginning the journey to understand Bitcoins, it is necessary to understand what cryptocurrency is and how it can and is changing the future of currencies and economy throughout the world.

You must have observed the boom of cryptocurrencies and how they seem to be everywhere nowadays, especially in the case of Bitcoins. If you want to learn about Bitcoins it is necessary to learn about cryptocurrencies first and to learn about cryptocurrencies first, it is necessary to learn about our regular or conventional currencies first. For instance, let's say that you have a $10 in your wallet. How do you know that the value of the bill is the same that is printed on it? How do we fix the value and how do we believe that the piece of paper is worth $10? How does society accept that the piece of paper is valuable and how does it become legitimate?

When we talk or think about currency, the first image that comes to our minds is of paper notes, metal coins, etc. However, this notion has been changing over a couple of decades now. Nowadays, we use cards and Internet banking where we do not have to come into contact with physical money or currency. The Bitcoin boom is in a way an advancement of this same principle.

A cryptocurrency is a form of digitized currency that is not physical and is intangible. It is available in an encrypted form in which the data is stored as well as transferred in the form of code. This code protects the currency from theft and hacking. Like our regular or fiat currency, cryptocurrency too only achieves or gains value when people or society assigns it a value. The value of Bitcoins is going up day by day. For instance, a single Bitcoin was worth a pound of gold in the mid-June 2017!

People often think that as cryptocurrency is in intangible form, it is not as valuable as other forms of currencies. However, this is a myth. There is no difference between cryptocurrencies and fiat currencies, just that the former is intangible while the later is tangible. Another factor that sets cryptocurrency apart from regular or fiat currency is that no authority such as a government, a bank or any other regulatory institution controls cryptocurrency. There are no fixed rules on how and why to use it. It is quite difficult to steal cryptocurrency thanks to the blockchain technique used by Bitcoins. From the above factors, it can be assumed that cryptocurrency is truly the freest of all the currencies in the world. This book will help you understand the basics of Bitcoins and will teach you how to invest in them.

Fluctuating Paper Currency

You saw a few questions asked in the last section of this chapter. Fiat currency or paper currency only becomes valuable when a value is defined or given to the currency by a central bank, a regulatory authority or a government. All the currencies that we use in our day to day lives are fiat or regular currencies. These include the US dollar, Pound, Yen, Rupees, etc. A fiat currency is only worth its purchasing power. However, there is no fixed standard for determining the purchasing power. This factor is responsible for various drawbacks. Let us see some of the drawbacks of fiat currency one by one.

Money is an abstraction. Abstraction is a part of the language that is used to describe a particular word. Compared to this, the abstract is a mental representation of an idea such as justice, equality, fraternity, etc. There exists a huge difference between abstract and abstraction. The abstract ideas are always used to explain ideas and thoughts that exist only in the human mind. The concept of money is in a way an abstraction while the value of the money is abstract. Money has no value of its own, and similarly, fiat money has no value of its own either. Once upon a time, the gold standard was used in the US to fixate value to money. However, it has been replaced by legal force. US citizens now accept the Federal Reserve notes in the place of the gold certificates. This acceptance is in a way coercion and the citizens were forced to accept this pressure.

It is assumed that one of the main reasons why we evolved was because we started trading. Trading plays an important role in our day-to-day lives. It is, in a way, an essential part of the survival of the human species. Trading is as natural as living for us. The desire and need to exchange valuable things for valuable objects allow us to live in the modern world. It is necessary to have voluntary arrangements and transactions in a marketplace, free of intermediaries who derive certain commission or rent in the process.

Fiat currency seems problematic because it is based on coercion. Forcing a developed society to accept artificial money, which has a fluctuating and uncertain value is a risk that has been forced on people. Fiat currency is also risky because it allows the person who controls the currency to control the power as well. This allows the redistribution of wealth to happen by a simple alteration of quantity and availability.

The central authority has the power of establishing a complete and totalitarian monopoly on the currency that it issues and also has the power of eliminating any other form of currency that seems like a competition to its currency. Human beings are prone to mistakes, and the people who control fiat currency can make errors as well. It is impossible to have perfect planning in the central economy, and it may lead to disastrous after-effects and consequences. This may lead to a problematic economy.

It is not possible to have price stability while using fiat currency. The price of fiat currency is unstable and may often lead to artificial depression. This is why Bitcoins and other forms of cryptocurrencies serve as a far better option than fiat or regular currency.

Chapter Two: Bitcoin: The Basics

Before looking at how you can use and invest in Bitcoins, it is necessary to understand a brief history of the same. This will allow you to appreciate the journey of Bitcoin and see how it revolutionizes the economy.

History:

The history of Bitcoins is as interesting as the coins itself. An anonymous software developer who was later revealed to be Satoshi Nakamoto was the first person to develop Bitcoins. Satoshi wanted to develop Bitcoins because he wanted to provide an electronic payment system that was based on mathematical equations. He wanted to create a currency that was not centralized and which could be transferred electronically with ease.

Nakamoto published a paper titled as "Bitcoin: A Peer-to-Peer Electronic Cash System" which is often seen as the birth of the Bitcoins. In this paper, a variety of methods of using a peer-to-peer system to generate a financial transaction without the need of any middlemen was explained in details. This paper was published in the year 2009, and the same year marks the birth of Bitcoins. The paper led to the formation of the first open source Bitcoin client, and later Bitcoins were issued for the first time. Nakamoto was the first person to mine the first block of Bitcoins, and he acquired 50 Bitcoins as a reward for it. After Nakamoto, Hal Finney was the second person who downloaded and utilized the Bitcoin client for which he received 10 Bitcoins from Satoshi as a reward. This is known as the first Bitcoin transaction in the world. However, soon users found a loophole or a weak spot in the Bitcoin protocol. They found that transaction on the network could be verified even before they were entered in the blockchain network. Due to this, the users were able to potentially bypass the economic restrictions surrounding Bitcoins and then create an infinite amount of Bitcoins. This would have diluted the value of Bitcoins. This was a severe loophole, and it had to be fixed as soon as possible to secure the future of Bitcoins.

The loophole mentioned above was exploited on the 15th of August in the year 2010 when somebody created more than 184 billion Bitcoins, which then were forwarded to two different networks of Bitcoins. The loophole was fixed soon, and thus the above case is the only case of lapse related to the Bitcoin system since its launch in the year 2009

The discovery or invention of Bitcoins started showing its effects almost immediately. WikiLeaks and other such companies started accepting donations in the form of Bitcoins. The financial system started gaining popularity all over the world very soon afterward. Around 2011, various videos regarding Bitcoins were uploaded on the Internet, and many of them went viral as well. In 2011, another important event happened in the history of Bitcoins as Vitalik Buterin co-founded a new magazine, which deals with Bitcoins, and Bitcoin related issues only. By 2012, around 1000 merchants around the world had started accepting Bitcoins as a valid currency.

What is a Bitcoin?

Bitcoin is considered to be the first cryptocurrency invented. It is held and stored in a digital form. The currency is represented with the help of a long code, and a well-connected and extensive network of miners throughout the world monitors it. The Bitcoin users and the miners both have to solve different levels of codes to access and generate Bitcoins or other forms of cryptocurrencies. Bitcoin is a self-contained currency that is available in a digitized form that enables you to store it on your own without involving a third party. Bitcoins are almost like gold coins or bullion and can work like any other form of regular currency as well. Although often compared to gold, Bitcoins have now become even more expensive than gold. Around mid of July 2017, a single Bitcoin was valued around at $2600.

Bitcoins are traded using wallets, and as it is a private database, it is possible to store it on hard drives, memory sticks or even in the cloud. Bitcoins cannot be forged and thus are much safer and risk-free than regular fiat currency. As it needs a lot of effort as well as intensive computation to forge Bitcoins, the whole process ultimately turns out valueless. Bitcoin is a highly volatile currency as compared to fiat currencies and that often makes the value of Bitcoins unstable, so to be on the safe side it is always advised to check various sites before buying Bitcoins.

Bitcoins and related system are decentralized. Thus it has no regulatory authority to control it. The value of Bitcoins is determined by the necessity and the forces of demand and supply. No one has the power to manipulate the entire network of Bitcoins as miners are spread all over the world. All the transactions done using Bitcoins are in public information, and any miner can check the transaction or verify it anytime. This allows minders to monitor the transactions safely and to reduce the discrepancies that often creep into networks such as this. Miners are paid or rewarded (in Bitcoins) for each block of mined data.

Users can use Bitcoins to buy things electronically or on the web. This process is quite similar to the use of conventional currency on the Internet. However, the only thing that differentiates Bitcoins from conventional currencies is that there is not a controlling authority that regulates the network.

Who prints Bitcoins?

The most frequently asked question about Bitcoins is who prints them. In reality, no one prints Bitcoins, as they are not available in a tangible form, rather, people mine them. As it is a form of digital currency, no central authority can print them. Governments and banks often print new money to cover national debt. However, this often devaluates the currency. In the Bitcoins system, there is no central authority, which is why anyone in the world can join them for free. It is possible to mine Bitcoins using the distributed network.

Fiat or regular currency is often based on one precious metal or another, which means that the amount of money that you hold in your pocket is equal to its face value in gold. However, this is only true in the case of fiat currency. Bitcoins are free of this concept and bondage. Bitcoins instead combine a set lengthy equations and users around the world use various software to solve these codes to mine Bitcoins. When this transaction is verified successfully, the amount gets added to the blockchain, which can be later confirmed by anyone. Anyone can access the blockchain as it is based on open source code.

Features of a Bitcoin

As said earlier, Bitcoins are not controlled or regulated by any centralized authority and that makes Bitcoins decentralized. Any machine with enough computing power can mine Bitcoins and can also successfully process the transactions that are present on the network. All such devices work together to keep the system from sinking. As the system works with combined effort, no single user can take over the system.

Almost every individual in the world has a bank account. You must remember how difficult and cumbersome it is to open a new bank account and how much time it needs. However, the process of opening a Bitcoin account is quite simple. You can set up a Bitcoin account for free and that too in no time. It is also safe and secure as the network guarantees anonymity. It is also possible to have multiple accounts or addresses per user, and these addresses are not linked to names or any other kind of personal data either. The overall system, as well as the network, is transparent and every transaction is recorded in the blockchain ledger. If you decide to make your Bitcoin address public, the number of Bitcoins you hold will be visible to everyone. However, your identity will not be visible. It is also possible to protect your transactions as well as your identity while using the Bitcoin network.

The Bitcoin network is especially great for overseas transactions as the whole process is free. Normally, while making international transactions using the fiat currency, the bank levies a specific fee on the user. The overall transaction may also take a long time. However, in Bitcoin transactions, the whole process is not only free, but it is also quick and effortless. It does not involve any third party which makes it quite safe and secure as well.

Bitcoin investing strategies

In this section let us go through some of the basic investing strategies and tips that you should be aware of before investing in Bitcoins.

Be Prepared:

It is necessary to be prepared and have a proper strategy if you want to succeed in life. Similarly, if you want to become a successful investor in Bitcoins or even fiat currency, it is necessary to have a strategy. You need to have a plan and should know why you want to invest in Bitcoins. Once you know the reason behind your interest in Bitcoins, it will allow you to form a proper framework that will enable to continue your transactions risk-free.

Prices will fluctuate:

As said earlier, the price of Bitcoins are extremely volatile, and it is bound to fluctuate often. The price of Bitcoins can drop like other investments often. The price drops in this system are far more frequent and quicker than other systems as it is a volatile form of investment. It is necessary to understand that the prices of your Bitcoins will change often. Similarly, it is quite difficult to understand the future of Bitcoins. However, looking at the speed Bitcoins are growing, it can be safely said that Bitcoins will become our main currency soon.

Secure Your Bitcoins:

What makes Bitcoins one of the best currencies in the world is that you are in full control of all of your funds. However, this extra power also brings in extra responsibility. You need to understand that only you are responsible for your funds and even a tiny error may ruin your finances. Always store your Bitcoins in a secure way to avoid serious losses.

How Do You Like The Book So Far?

CLICK HERE TO LEAVE FEEDBACK ON AMAZON

If you're undecided, just leave a review later...

Chapter Three: Buying Bitcoins

In the last chapter, you read all about the history and the basics of Bitcoins. Now it is time to understand how to invest in Bitcoins and how to use them. This chapter will extensively deal with how you can buy Bitcoins in a secure and risk-free way.

Bitcoin wallets

Wallets in real life are meant to keep your money safe. Similarly, in the Bitcoins terminology; wallets are 'systems' that keep your money from being stolen in exchange. Although Bitcoins are an extremely safe to use form of currency, the exchange does not take any responsibility for keeping your money safe, and the onus lies with you to keep your money in a safer place.

Every Bitcoin user is provided with a private key, and if you manage to lose this key, you will lose your money as well. As the system is decentralized, you will not be able to contact a customer service executive, as the service does not exist. It is your responsibility to keep everything related your money safe and secure. No one should be able to find your private key and should not be able to use it either. Some people tend to memorize their private key. However, writing it down in a safe place is a good option as well.

Remember, money once lost in Bitcoins cannot be recovered in any way. Do not choose an easy to use and download wallet as the ease of usability often leads to compromised and flimsy security features. These gaps in security features may result in loss of information. Do your research and only then select a wallet.

You can store Bitcoins in two types of wallets; these are cold wallets and hot wallets. Cold wallets are offline wallets, and they are not connected to the Internet in any way, whereas hot wallets are online wallets that exist or are connected to the Internet. Cold wallets are considered to be much safer than hot wallets as the latter can be hacked easily. Let us now go through a list of various wallets to choose from.

Desktop wallets

As the name suggests, desktop wallets are the wallets that can be downloaded to your computer or laptop. To download a desktop wallet, it is first necessary to download a Bitcoin client. These are written in Bitcoin languages, which makes it easier for the user to download and use them. Once you successfully install the wallet on your computer, you need to sync it with the blockchain transactions on the network.

Examples: Exodus, Bitcoin Core, and Electrum.

Mobile wallets

As the name suggests, these wallets can be downloaded onto your mobile phone. However, most of these wallets support only smartphones. These wallets are also known as lite-wallets, and you need to download secondary data to run and allow users to perform transactions.

Many users prefer mobile wallets because they find it easier to use as compared to the desktop wallets. However, mobile wallets have various security issues. People who use mobile wallets prefer to validate deals themselves, as they do not trust the middlemen.

One major feature of mobile wallets is that it can be used with a QR code feature where you just need to scan the QR code of the receiver to send the money or vice versa.

Another feature of this type of wallet is that you can use it as a cold storage option as well. You can store the private key in a phone that you do not regularly use to keep your key safe.

These wallets are quite flexible, and they allow you to add infinite amount of Bitcoins.

Hardware wallets

Hardware wallets are physical wallets that are also known as nano ledgers. These wallets are made in such a way that they combine the features of mobile as well as desktop wallets. These hybrid wallets are safe and allow the users to keep the money away from the Internet. You can also access your data without being connected to the Internet and can go through the transactions with ease. You can carry these wallets around with you and can keep them safe. They are a bit pricey as compared to other wallets. However, the price is justified, as they are much safer as well.

Examples: Trezor and Ledger HW.1

Paper wallets

Paper wallets are simply a piece of paper on which you write down your private key to keep it safe. You can place this key wherever you want. It is one of the best ways of storing keys as it highly safe and are less likely to lose them.

This is the best form of cold storage as no hacker can hack this method thus making theft impossible. Whenever you want to do a transaction, just remove the key from your safe place, perform the transaction and replace the key. However, it is necessary to keep this key safe as a key once lost cannot be traced back and you will lose all your money.

What are keys?

Keys are the codes that are assigned to your currency that gives it a unique identity. This allows you to make transactions with ease. Codes are one of the most important aspects related to Bitcoins and other cryptocurrencies as well.

Keys are in a way the numbers that are present on your debit or credit card. As these numbers provide your credit or debit cards a unique identity, similarly, the keys provide your currency a unique identity as well. They will allow you to transfer money to your wallet.

Keys are made up of a set of alphanumeric series. There are two types of keys, private and public, and both these need to work together to make a transaction. The private key, as the name suggests is your key that should not be shared with anyone. It should be kept safe and should only be used when you want to make a transaction. The public key is shared with those you want to transact with. Both the public and private keys need to match if you want to make a successful transaction.

When you buy Bitcoins, the keys will be generated automatically, and you cannot choose your numbers.

Bitcoin exchanges

There are a variety of Bitcoin exchanges to choose from. Most of these exchanges are like bank accounts where you can store your digital as well as fiat currencies. If you are interested in trading Bitcoins, exchanges will prove to be a great option for you.

Opening an account on these exchanges is quite easy, and you do not need to follow a lot of steps or go through lengthy procedures to do so. Similarly, you do not need to disclose your personal information if you wish to transact on an exchange. The rules governing the exchanges are the same throughout the world. No exchange holds the power to confiscate Bitcoins from any user. You can choose any exchange you want. However, it is recommended to choose an exchange that is closest to your location.

Some of the most commonly used Bitcoin exchanges include Bitfinex based in Hong Kong, Bitstamp in the US, BTC-e, Kraken based in the US, Huobi in China and Hong Kong, OK-Coin and BTCC based in China, and Coinbase.

Once you have successfully created an account, just link it to your bank and make the required arrangements to perform transfers successfully.

One-on-one meeting

If you prefer anonymity and do not want to go into the hassles of banking and such, you can buy Bitcoins from local sellers as well. However, this is only possible if you live in a large city. You can find more about such transactions on websites like the LocalBitcoins. These sites can be used to fix meetings with Bitcoin traders, and you can decide whether you want to finalize the transaction or not.

If you do decide to choose this method of buying Bitcoins, it is necessary to have instant access to your wallet along with a good Internet connection.

You should take certain precautions while buying Bitcoins using this method. Always meet your trader in a public place. Never carry a lot of cash with you when you go to meet a trader, especially if the trader is new. If you do not like one-on-one meetings, there are certain websites where you can arrange group buying and selling meetings as well.

Mining Bitcoins

The most well-known and trusted way of acquiring Bitcoins is mining. To become a miner, you need to have a dedicated computer along with a powerful graphics card. Nowadays, mining is done in pools, i.e., a couple of miners get together, group their resources and then mine for Bitcoins. At the end of the process, the resultant Bitcoins are divided among all the involved parties. You will find more information regarding this concept in the next chapter.

Investment trust

If you do not want to buy and store a lot of Bitcoins, you can also invest in investment trusts such as Bitcoin Investment Trust or BIT. This process is similar to mutual funds.

Bitcoin ATMs

This is a new concept. However, it is becoming popular rapidly. This method is the one-on-one method. However, instead of another user, you get your money from a machine. Just scan your QR code or insert your currency and the machine will generate a code for loading Bitcoins in your wallet.

Buying Bitcoins is a very simple process. However, you may feel a bit overwhelmed at first. Don't worry; with enough practice you will be able to make transactions using Bitcoins in no time.

Chapter Four: Bitcoin Mining

In the last chapter, you saw the various kinds of Bitcoin wallets and how you can buy Bitcoins with ease. You also saw a brief introduction to Bitcoin mining in the last chapter. However, the topic is quite extensive and forms the core of Bitcoins. This chapter will try to cover Bitcoin mining in detail and will also give tips on how to start mining on your own.

Mining Bitcoin

As said earlier, Bitcoins are generated by mining. It is possible to generate as many Bitcoins as you want. However, there exists a global limit on Bitcoins. A limit of 21 million has been set on Bitcoins out of which about half of the Bitcoins have already been mined.

Unlike fiat or regular currencies, Bitcoins cannot be issued by government, banks or any such authority. Thus, there is no regulation on the production Bitcoins. You need to solve a variety of extremely complex equations to mine Bitcoins. The process is quite intense, and it needs a lot of resources. The number of people looking to mine Bitcoins has increased drastically in the last couple of years. With increasing competition, the equations to are becoming difficult as well.

A person needs to have a good mining rig as well as ample time if they want to mine Bitcoins. As said earlier, it requires a lot of resources as well. For instance, you may require a lot of electricity to mine Bitcoins. The overall cost of the process is quite high, and thus professionals often do Bitcoin mining only. As the system needs to work continuously for a couple of days in Bitcoin mining, you need to have an efficient cooling system as well. As the costs involved in the process are high, many miners often pool their resources to extract Bitcoins.

The resultant Bitcoins are then divided among the participants.

Bitcoin Blockchain

The government is responsible for printing conventional money. However, as said earlier, Bitcoins cannot be printed, and they must be discovered. Nowadays, users all around the world compete with each other to discover and mine these Bitcoins. The Bitcoin network is also used to transfer Bitcoins around the world as well. The network is anonymous unless someone is keeping track of the transactions from the beginning.

The Bitcoin network collects data regarding the transactions that happen in a given period and then compiles it in a list. This list is a block. A miner then confirms these transactions and then notes them in a ledger. Various blocks form a ledger, and various ledgers form a blockchain. An entry can be only noted down when the transaction takes place between two Bitcoin addresses. When a new list is created, it is directly added to an existing blockchain. This often results in a long list of transactions. Every miner receives an alert whenever something is updated on the block.

The ledger is quite safe even though the data is held in a digital form. Miners put blocks of transactions through various specific processes. A mathematical code is applied to the data in the block in this process. Thus, the block gets transformed into a different form resulting in the production of a hash, which is a short and random sequence of numbers and text. This hash is kept at the end of the blockchain network. It is quite simple to make a hash from the data that is available. However, it is quite difficult to identify which data was used to form the hash. All hashes are unique, and if even a single character is

24

changed in a hash, the whole blockchain will be changed as well.

All transactions that are recorded in the block are responsible for the generation of hash. Each new block on the chain will be based on the hash of the previous block. This sequence forms a seal that cannot be changed or broken without alarming all the miners present in a network. Even if a tiny alteration is made, every miner will be alerted.

Start mining

Bitcoins are gaining rapid popularity throughout the world. The recent boom has made everyone aware of the power of Bitcoins, which is why everyone wants to invest in them. This has resulted in increased competition in the world of Bitcoins. Similarly, the competition in the field of Bitcoin mining is increasing rapidly as well. The hardware that is used for mining has evolved as well. If you want to get into mining, it is necessary to invest in good equipment and hardware. You can buy the hardware according to your budget as well as expected profit. If you expect to get a lot of profit, you will have to spend a lot of money on hardware as well. With some tinkering, it is possible to use a regular graphics card for Bitcoin mining. When Bitcoins are mined using GPU instead of CPU the productivity of the coins increases as well.

Nowadays, miners use the FPGA system to mine Bitcoins. The FPGA system or field programmable gate array is a combination of the power of CPU and GPU. However, it consumes much less electricity as compared to them. Another revolutionary and widely used technology to mine Bitcoins is the Bitcoin ASICs. This technology is currently the best technology to mine Bitcoins.

It is necessary to understand that Bitcoin mining is not a simple and quick process. It takes a lot of time to mine Bitcoins. Similarly, it takes a lot of resources such as electricity, time and money to mine Bitcoins. So, unless you are a professional with professional equipment and enough resources to spare, do not take up Bitcoin mining.

Chapter Five: Pros and Cons of Bitcoins

Bitcoins are rapidly gaining popularity throughout the world. Bitcoins are a highly beneficial form of currency. In this chapter let us go through the pros and cons of Bitcoins.

Inflation risk

Inflation is price rise where the price of commodities rises. In this situation, the money loses its power as new notes are pumped into circulation by the governing authority. This is a highly common problem in the case of fiat or regular currency. However, this is problem is almost non-existent in the case of Bitcoins. As Bitcoins are decentralized and are not controlled by any single authority, they cannot cause inflation.

It is believed that by the end of 2050, one Bitcoin will cater at least 500 people around the world. There is no looming danger of spending all the money, and thus there is no danger of inflation as well.

Failure

One of the biggest problems associated with the introduction of new currency is the fear of failure. The new currency is often susceptible to failure. However the same cannot be said about Bitcoins. Bitcoins are quite safe, and they already hold an important place in the world of virtual currencies. They cannot fail as they are decentralized. You do not need to worry about the changes in the rules and regulations of the government or central authority. The value of Bitcoins will not drop overnight or it will not be demonetized suddenly. Bitcoin is a stable form of currency, and it is not influenced by new regulations and rules.

Safety

People are often quite concerned when they need to invest online. Security is the primary concern of a person who wants to invest online. People often think twice before they decide to invest. This fear is valid as there have been various scams that fooled many users and looted them of their hard earned money. However, Bitcoins and trading in Bitcoins are extremely safe, if done through a good and trustworthy sources. The Bitcoin system uses the blockchain system which is quite safe and with no chance of fraudulent activity. It provides buyers' protection. This protection is also applied to the sellers thus providing two-way security.

Portability

One of the best things about Bitcoins is that they are highly portable. You can carry millions of dollars-worth of Bitcoins in your pocket without any stress or problem. Just try imagining doing the same with regular dollars. As Bitcoins are intangible, no one will suspect you or try to steal it from you when you carry the money. Bitcoins are always safe because they cannot be accessed without a private key. These factors make Bitcoins extremely risk-free as well as stress-free for the users.

No tracing

Bitcoins allow you to stay anonymous almost all of the time. For instance, when you send money to a seller or buyer, they will get the money. However, they will not be able to trace it back to you. This feature keeps your identity safe and prevents your account from being traced. This means that no government, bank, company or any such authority or figure will be able to track your investment and wallets. This allows Bitcoins to be the freest currency in the world as it can protect you from identity theft and allow you to make transactions with ease.

Growth

One of the unique features of Bitcoins that we are witnessing nowadays is its tendency to grow. The value of Bitcoins will continue to grow which is not the case with fiat or regular money. If you buy a thousand dollars-worth of Bitcoin today, their value will surely go up after some time. However, if you keep the same amount of fiat money in a bank or safe, its value will not go up. Bitcoins are just like silver or gold; their value will continue to rise with time.

Global

Bitcoin is the true global currency as it can be bought, sold and exchanged throughout the world for services as well as commodities. So, it is possible to buy Bitcoin in the USA, then exchange it in Japan and then use it in Europe for services or vice versa. Due to its global nature and ease of use, Bitcoin is preferred by many over fiat currencies.

Real-world applications

Many people often discard Bitcoins as having no value in the real world. However, this is just a myth; Bitcoins have several real-world applications as well. You do not need to wait a long time to reap the benefits of Bitcoins; you can start using them immediately. You can use Bitcoins in your day-to-day life once you buy them. You can even use them to buy daily objects such buying groceries and other such essentials.

Transactions costs

Another major benefit of Bitcoins is that the cost of transaction is quite small as compared to regular transactions. You do not need to buy and sell a lot of Bitcoins to buy goods and services, as there exists no intermediary in the transaction. As there is no intermediary in the transaction, you do not need to shell out any commission, just a tiny fraction of the amount will be used for transaction costs, and that is it.

Taxes

Bitcoins are not taxed in the regular sense. No one can trace the Bitcoin transactions, and no one can know where the coins come from. It is difficult to trace the source of any transaction. This is quite suitable for anyone who wants to avoid paying a lot of taxes.

Transparency

The Bitcoin system is one of the most transparent systems in the world, and no unwarranted charges can pass through the system. A seller cannot make any alteration without it being noticed and subsequently recorded on the ledger. This transparency makes Bitcoin one of the safest currencies in the world. People feel more confident about investing into Bitcoin thanks to the amount of security and transparency it offers.

These are some of the advantages that make Bitcoin one of the best forms of currency in the world.

Disadvantages:

Bitcoin is one of the most revolutionary and beneficial currencies in the world. It is quite clear how useful Bitcoins can be from the above characteristics. However, Bitcoins do have some cons and problems associated with them, albeit most of them are just myths. Let us try to answer and look at some of the problems associated with Bitcoins in this section.

Irreversible Transactions

One of the major disadvantages of Bitcoins is that the transactions are permanent and they cannot be reversed. If you accidentally send someone a few coins by mistakes, you will never be able to recover them. Most of the fiat currency transactions do not have this problem. It is, therefore, necessary to be quite careful while dealing with Bitcoins and making transactions using them. Always authorize transactions personally.

Competition

Many new forms of cryptocurrency have now come out that are comparatively lighter than Bitcoins. These new forms of currencies include the highly popular Ether and Ripple. These are not only cheaper but also faster as compared to Bitcoins. It is possible that they may takeover Bitcoins in the future. However, for now, Bitcoins are leading the world of cryptocurrencies, and they are expected to rule to market for a while.

Thus, these were the benefits as well as cons of investing into Bitcoins.

Conclusion

I would like to thank you once again for purchasing this book, and I hope it proved to be an informative as well as entertaining read.

Bitcoin is rapidly becoming one of the most talked about topics in the world. People are talking about it, and everyone wants to invest in it. However, for an unaccustomed person, the world of Bitcoins may seem to be quite difficult, confusing and daunting. This book will help you solve all the questions that you have in your mind about Bitcoins and will serve as a 'how to' guide that will help you become rich using Bitcoins in no time.

This book also covers the basics of Bitcoins such as the history of Bitcoins and its benefits over other currencies. The book also covered the blockchain technology and how you can mine for Bitcoins. It is necessary to understand that Bitcoins are here to stay and, perhaps shortly, they will become the main currency of the world. It is always better to be prepared well in advance. This book will have helped you to learn everything there is to know about Bitcoins in a simple, jargon-free language.

Once again thank you for buying this book and all the best!

And finally, if you liked the book, I would like to ask you to do me a favor and leave a review for the book on Amazon. Just go to your account on Amazon or click on the link below.

CLICK HERE TO LEAVE A REVIEW ON AMAZON!

Thank you and good luck!

www.ingramcontent.com/pod-product-compliance
Lightning Source LLC
Chambersburg PA
CBHW071201220526
45468CB00003B/1118